# Plants Can Bite!

Calling all aliens!
Are you planning a holiday to planet Earth?
Finn and Zeek are here to help.

'Plants Can Bite!'
Published by MAVERICK ARTS PUBLISHING LTD

Suite 1, Hillreed House, 54 Queen Street,
Horsham, RH13 5AD, +44 (0)1403 256941
© Maverick Arts Publishing Limited August 2024

A CIP catalogue record for this book is available at the British Library.

ISBN 978-1-83511-013-3

Printed in India

www.maverickbooks.co.uk

Credits:
Finn & Zeek illustrations by Jake McDonald, Bright Illustration Agency
Cover: Jake McDonald/Bright, © Kuttelvaserova Stuchelova/Shutterstock
Inside: © Linas T/Shutterstock (6), © Simon Groewe/Shutterstock (7), © FabrikaSimf/Shutterstock (7), © Tatiana Bralnina/Shutterstock (8), © Anna Yakymenko/Shutterstock (9), © Steve Bower/Shutterstock (10), © all_about_people/Shutterstock (11), © Nakornthai/Shutterstock (12-13), © Linas T/Shutterstock (14), © Linas T/Shutterstock (14), © Mara Fribus/Shutterstock (15), © Kira Volkov/Shutterstock (16), © Oksana_Schmidt/Shutterstock (17), © Roman Mikhailiuk/Shutterstock (18), © Alex Veresovich/Shutterstock (18), © martin.dlugo/Shutterstock (19), © London photographer HFT94/Shutterstock (19), © Fabrizio Guarisco/Shutterstock (20), © Simon Groewe/Shutterstock (20), © Arsgera/Shutterstock (21), © Olha Solodenko/Shutterstock (21), © Ilyshev Dmitry/Shutterstock (22), © BestPhotoStudio/Shutterstock (23), © Angel DiBilio/Shutterstock (23), © Matthew J Thomas/Shutterstock (24-25), © Kelly vanDellen/Shutterstock (27), © London photographer HFT94/Shutterstock (28)

This book is rated as: Turquoise Band (Guided Reading)

# Plants Can Bite!

## Contents

| | |
|---|---|
| Introduction | 6 |
| Carnivorous Plants | 8 |
|     Snap Traps | 10 |
|     Pitfall Traps | 12 |
|     Sticky Traps | 14 |
| Poisonous Plants | 16 |
|     Common | 18 |
|     Deadly! | 20 |
| Self-Defence Experts | 22 |
| Conclusion | 24 |
| Quiz | 28 |
| Index/Glossary | 30 |

# INCOMING MESSAGE

Dear Finn and Zeek,

We have heard that some of the plant life on Earth can be a little scary and that some can even bite!

What should we look out for when we visit?

From,
Stig and Pol
*(Planet Sneezle)*

# Introduction

Some plant life on Earth can be dangerous. Dangerous plants can be split into different groups:

## Carnivorous Plants

*A horse-fly in a Venus flytrap*

# Poisonous Plants

*Deadly nightshade*

# Defensive Plants

*Cactus*

# Carnivorous Plants

A carnivorous plant is one that is meat-eating! They are found all around the world, usually in damp places where there are not many **nutrients** in the soil.

Each plant has its own way of trapping its prey. There are different types of traps.

Poor fly!

# Carnivorous Plants   Snap Traps

The most famous snap trap is the Venus flytrap. They have leaves that look like mouths with tiny hairs inside.

They attract a fly onto their leaves by creating a fruit-like smell. The fly's movement triggers the little hairs, then SNAP! The trap shuts! It does this in a blink of an eye.

The plant then uses **enzymes** to kill its prey and sucks out all its nutrients. Once it is finished, the trap will open again, ready for its next victim.

# Carnivorous Plants   Pitfall Traps

These are plants that have leaves that form a pit (a bit like a stomach). This pit has **toxic** liquid in it, which the plant uses to **digest** its dinner.

Its prey is drawn to the rim of the pit by the smell of nectar.

The rim is slippery and the prey can slide in.

Once inside, the prey is trapped in the pit!

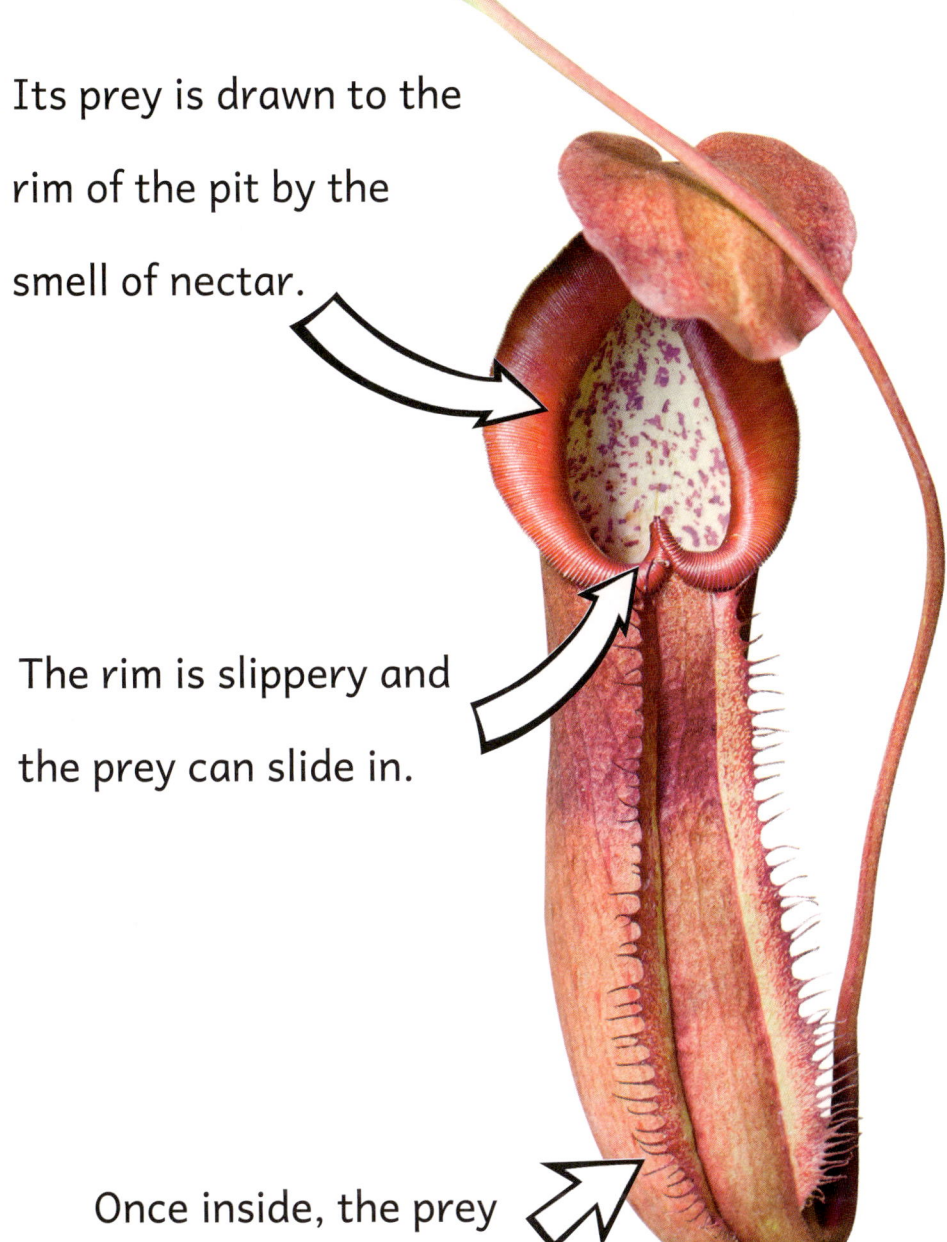

# Carnivorous Plants  Sticky Traps

These plants create a sticky glue.

Any prey that lands on the glue gets stuck and then is slowly digested!

# Poisonous Plants

Plants can't run away, but some of them can defend themselves from predators by being poisonous (either to touch or to eat). What may be poisonous to humans may not be to another animal.

**Laburnum is pretty but very poisonous!**

For a human, touching some poisonous plants can give you a bad rash or burns.

Eating a poisonous plant could give you a stomach ache or even be deadly!

So don't eat any plants without expert advice.

# Poisonous Plants  Common

Poisonous plants can be found everywhere, even near your house.

Here's a few you may find near where you live:

**Lily of the Valley**

All parts of this pretty plant are poisonous if eaten.

**Fly Agaric Mushroom**

Many mushrooms are poisonous but this one is especially toxic.

**Daffodils**

Yes, even the common daffodil is toxic if eaten!

**Foxgloves**

Beautiful but deadly if eaten. Keep an eye on any pets around them.

# Poisonous Plants — Deadly!

These are some of the deadliest plants in the world!

**Deadly nightshade** even sounds dangerous! All of it is poisonous to humans. However the berries are particularly dangerous as they look quite yummy! DO NOT EAT THEM.

**Tobacco** (which cigarettes are made from) is actually one of the most dangerous plants. Smoking tobacco kills many people each year.

**Poison hemlock** may look like common cow parsley, but beware: this plant can be dangerous to even touch.

# Self-Defence Experts

Some plants have other ways to defend themselves against being eaten.

**Sharp Spines/Thorns**

These can protect a plant from being touched or eaten by animals. Spiky!

*Cactus*

## Stingers

Some plants can sting when touched. Ouch!

*Stinging nettle*

## Getting Help

Some plants give food so that bugs will protect them. Isn't that clever?

*Bull horn tree*

## Conclusion

Plants are beautiful and fascinating! But you should always be careful never to touch or eat toxic plants. If unsure, leave well alone!

If you or someone you are with gets ill from a dangerous plant, you should call for an ambulance.

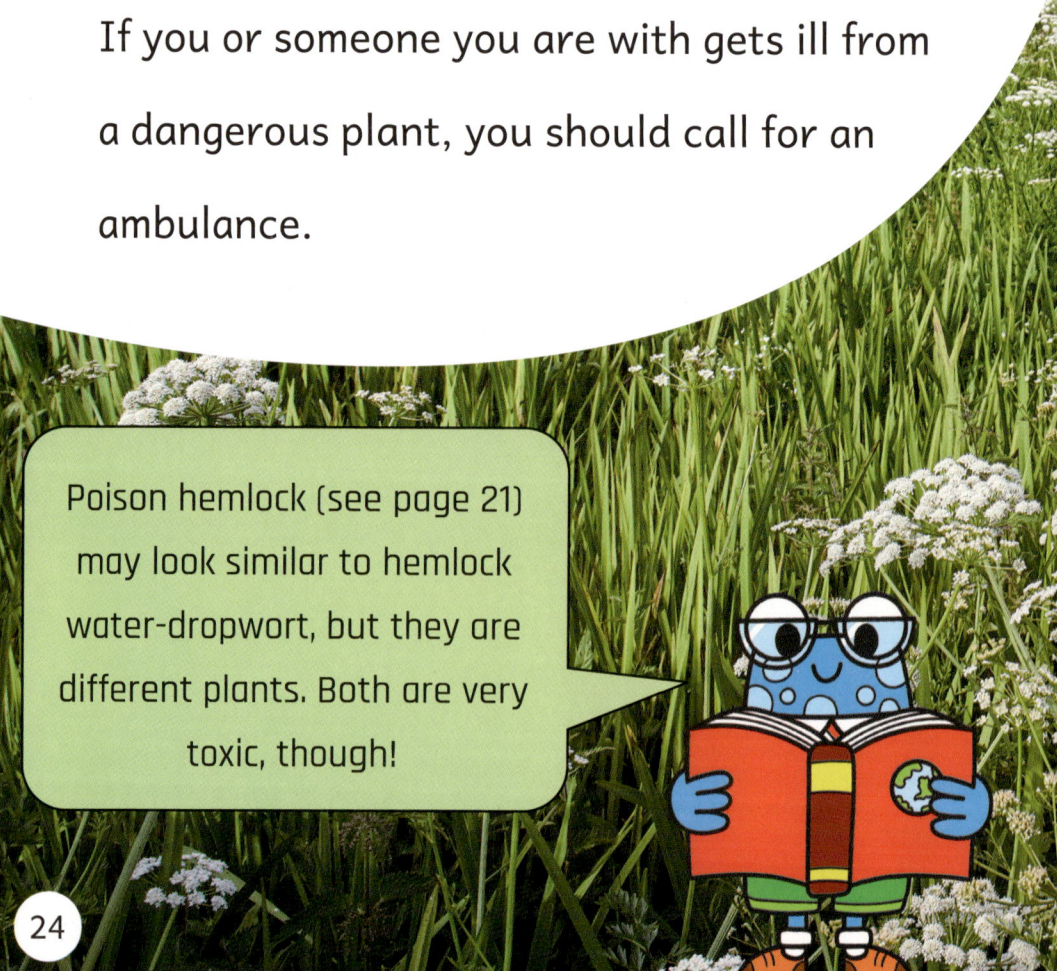

Poison hemlock (see page 21) may look similar to hemlock water-dropwort, but they are different plants. Both are very toxic, though!

# MESSAGE SENT

Dear Stig and Pol,

As you can see, there are some dangerous plants that can be found on Earth. However, if you are careful, they are easy to avoid.

Don't eat or touch anything without expert advice and you will be fine!

From,
Finn and Zeek :)

Look at the needles on this prickly pear cactus!

# Quiz

1. What do carnivorous plants eat?
a) Moss
b) Meat
c) Cheese

2. Name a famous snap trap plant.
a) Cactus
b) Deadly nightshade
c) Venus flytrap

3. Which poisonous plant is this?
a) Deadly nightshade
b) Daffodil
c) Foxglove

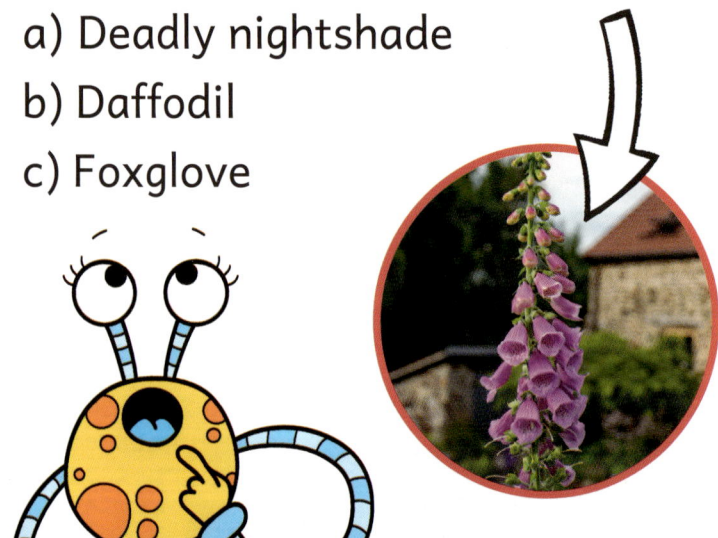

4. How does a cactus defend itself?
a) A snap trap
b) Sharp spines
c) Poison

5. What do sticky trap plants use to catch their prey?
a) Sharp spines
b) Sticky glue
c) A pitfall trap

6. What does poison hemlock look similar to?
a) Foxglove
b) Deadly nightshade
c) Hemlock water-dropwort

# Index/Glossary

**Carnivorous** pg 6, 8, 10, 12, 14
Something which eats meat.

**Nutrients** pg 8, 15
Substances which help living things to grow and be healthy.

**Toxic** pg 10, 18, 19, 24, 25
Something which is poisonous and harmful.

**Digest** pg 10, 13
When food is broken down and the nutrients in it are absorbed.

**Enzymes** pg 15
Substances which trigger certain chemical reactions.

*Quiz Answers:*

1. b, 2. c, 3. c, 4. b, 5. b, 6. c

## Helpful Symbols and their Meanings

 **Toxic**

 **Do not eat**

 **Danger**

 **Do not touch**

# Book Bands for Guided Reading

The Institute of Education book banding system is a scale of colours that reflects the various levels of reading difficulty. The bands are assigned by taking into account the content, the language style, the layout and phonics. Word, phrase and sentence level work is also taken into consideration.

Maverick Early Readers are a bright, attractive range of books covering the pink to white bands. All of these books have been book banded for guided reading to the industry standard and edited by a leading educational consultant.

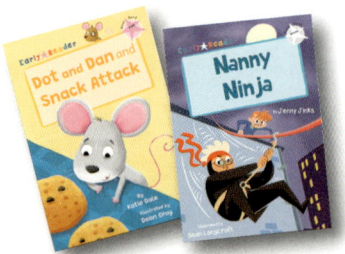

Fiction

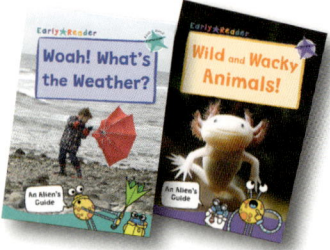

Non-fiction

To view the whole Maverick Readers scheme, visit our website at www.maverickearlyreaders.com

Or scan the QR code above to view our scheme instantly!